400+ Thrilling & Unbelievable Tank Facts for Military Enthusiasts

Explore Legendary Tank Commanders, Armored Feats, Cutting-Edge Technology & Much More! (The Ultimate Gift for Tank Fans & History Buffs)

Ethan Blackwell

CONTENTS

INTRODUCTION

Welcome to the captivating world of "400+ Thrilling & Unbelievable Tank Facts for Military Enthusiasts"—an extraordinary journey through the history, technology, and unforgettable moments of armored warfare. This comprehensive guidebook is designed to entertain, educate, and inspire tank enthusiasts, history buffs, and anyone with a fascination for these awe-inspiring machines.

As you delve into these pages, you'll discover a treasure trove of fascinating facts and anecdotes that showcase the evolution and impact of tanks on the battlefield. From the early days of lumbering World War I behemoths to the cutting-edge designs of modern main battle tanks, this book covers a wide range of topics that will keep you engrossed and amazed.

Across 20 engaging chapters, you'll explore the iconic tank models and their variants, the remarkable feats of armored units, and the groundbreaking technological advancements that have shaped tank warfare. You'll be captivated by stories of legendary tank commanders, dynamic duels, and the camaraderie forged among tank crews in the heat of battle.

But "400+ Thrilling & Unbelievable Tank Facts for Military Enthusiasts" is more than just a collection of facts and figures.

It's a celebration of human ingenuity, bravery, and the enduring spirit of those who have served in armored units throughout history. Through these pages, you'll gain a deeper appreciation for the crucial role tanks have played in shaping the course of conflicts and the sacrifices made by the men and women who operate them.

Whether you're a military history enthusiast, a tank aficionado, or simply someone with a thirst for knowledge, this book has something for everyone. You'll be amazed by the incredible stories of innovation and heroism, the quirky anecdotes and superstitions, and the artistic representations of tanks in popular culture.

So, dear reader, prepare to embark on an unforgettable journey through the world of armored warfare. Let "400+ Thrilling & Unbelievable Tank Facts for Military Enthusiasts" be your guide as you explore the triumphs and challenges, the past and future, of these incredible machines and the brave individuals who have operated them.

Get ready to be inspired, informed, and entertained as you uncover the fascinating stories and trivia that make the world of tanks truly captivating. Your adventure awaits, and the pages ahead are filled with surprises, revelations, and a newfound appreciation for the mighty armored vehicles that have left an indelible mark on military history.

EARLY HISTORY OF ARMORED VEHICLES

1. Leonardo da Vinci's Tank Design: In the late 15th century, Leonardo da Vinci sketched designs for a "tank" resembling a large armored vehicle with cannons protruding from its sides. While never built, da Vinci's design demonstrated early concepts of mobile artillery and armored protection.

2. First Recorded Use of Armored Vehicles: During the Renaissance period, armored wagons were employed in battle, featuring protective coverings made of metal plates or hardened leather to shield soldiers from enemy projectiles. These early armored vehicles provided rudimentary protection on the battlefield.

3. Turtle Ship of Korea: In the 16th century, Korean Admiral Yi Sun-sin developed the "turtle ship," a heavily armored naval vessel designed to withstand enemy attacks and intimidate adversaries with its formidable appearance. The turtle ship played a crucial role in defending Korea against Japanese invasion attempts.

4. Siege Towers and Battering Rams: Throughout ancient history, siege warfare often involved the use of armored siege towers and battering rams to breach enemy fortifications. These mobile structures provided protection for soldiers and allowed them to approach enemy walls while under fire.

5. Ironclad Warships of the Civil War: During the American Civil War, ironclad warships revolutionized naval warfare with their armored hulls and steam-powered engines. The USS Monitor and the CSS Virginia (Merrimack) famously battled in the first clash of ironclads at the Battle of Hampton Roads in 1862.

6. Medieval Knight Armor: Knights of the Middle Ages wore suits of armor made from steel plates to protect themselves in combat. These suits, consisting of helmets, breastplates, gauntlets, and greaves, provided exceptional protection against swords, arrows, and other weapons of the time.

7. Roman Testudo Formation: The Roman army utilized the "testudo" or tortoise formation during sieges and assaults, where soldiers interlocked their shields to form a protective shell over their heads. This formation provided cover from enemy projectiles and allowed Roman troops to advance safely.

8. Cataphracts of Ancient Persia: Ancient Persian cataphracts were heavily armored cavalry units equipped with lances, swords, and bows. Clad in scale armor or chainmail and riding

armored horses, cataphracts served as shock troops and played a significant role in ancient battles.

9. Chariots of Ancient Empires: Ancient civilizations such as Egypt, Assyria, and Persia employed armored chariots in warfare, featuring wooden frames covered with leather or metal plates for protection. These mobile platforms allowed archers and spearmen to engage enemies while remaining relatively safe.

10. Mongol Horse Archers: The Mongol Empire utilized highly mobile cavalry forces, including horse archers equipped with composite bows and leather lamellar armor. Mongol horsemen excelled at hit-and-run tactics, harassing enemy formations with volleys of arrows while evading retaliation.

11. Greek Phalanx: The ancient Greek phalanx formation consisted of heavily armored infantry soldiers called hoplites, who formed a dense shield wall with overlapping shields to protect themselves and their comrades. This disciplined formation provided mutual protection and formidable offensive capabilities.

12. Hussite War Wagons: During the Hussite Wars of the 15th century, Czech rebels known as Hussites constructed war wagons with armored walls and mounted cannons, creating

mobile fortresses that could withstand enemy attacks and deliver devastating firepower.

13. Scythed Chariots of Ancient Warfare: Some ancient civilizations equipped chariots with scythe blades attached to the wheels, creating lethal weapons capable of mowing down infantry formations. Scythed chariots were used in battles by civilizations such as the Persians, Greeks, and Romans.

14. Samurai Armor of Feudal Japan: Samurai warriors in feudal Japan wore suits of armor made from lacquered plates or scales laced together with silk cords. Known as "yoroi" or "dō-maru," this armor provided protection in battle and symbolized the samurai's status and honor.

15. War Elephants of Antiquity: Armored war elephants were used by ancient civilizations, including the Persians, Carthaginians, and Indians, as formidable battlefield assets. Elephants were often equipped with metal or wooden armor and trained to trample enemy infantry and break enemy lines.

16. Roman Legionary Armor: Roman legionaries wore segmented armor known as "lorica segmentata," consisting of interlocking metal plates or strips fastened to leather straps. This iconic armor provided flexibility and protection for Roman soldiers during their conquests and campaigns.

17. Chinese Terracotta Warriors: The famous terracotta army of Qin Shi Huang, the first Emperor of China, included life-sized statues of armored warriors crafted from terracotta clay. These statues, buried with the emperor to protect him in the afterlife, showcase the intricacies of ancient Chinese armor and weaponry.

18. Napoleonic Cavalry Armor: During the Napoleonic Wars, cavalry units often wore breastplates and helmets for protection in battle. These armored cuirasses provided limited defense against musket fire and melee weapons, allowing cavalrymen to charge enemy lines with greater confidence.

19. Viking Shields and Helmets: Viking warriors relied on round shields made from wood and reinforced with iron or leather for protection in combat. Viking helmets, typically made from iron and featuring nose guards and cheek pieces, provided head protection during raids and battles.

20. Bronze Age Chariot Warfare: In ancient Mesopotamia, Egypt, and other civilizations of the Bronze Age, chariots played a crucial role in warfare, serving as mobile platforms for archers and spearmen. These early armored vehicles were instrumental in battles and conquests of the ancient world.

ICONIC TANK MODELS & THEIR VARIANTS

1. T-34: The Soviet T-34 medium tank, introduced during World War II, is widely regarded as one of the most influential tank designs in history. Its sloped armor, powerful 76mm gun, and robust construction made it a formidable adversary for German tanks on the Eastern Front.

2. M4 Sherman: The American M4 Sherman tank, named after Union General William Tecumseh Sherman, was the most widely used Allied tank during World War II. Its versatility, reliability, and mass production contributed significantly to Allied victory in Europe and the Pacific.

3. Panzerkampfwagen IV: The German Panzer IV medium tank served as the backbone of the Wehrmacht's armored forces during World War II. Initially intended as a support tank, it underwent numerous upgrades and variants throughout the war, remaining in production until 1945.

4. Centurion: The British Centurion main battle tank, introduced after World War II, was one of the most successful and long-lived

tank designs of the 20th century. It saw extensive service in conflicts such as the Korean War, the Vietnam War, and the Arab-Israeli conflicts.

5. Tiger I: The German Tiger I heavy tank, introduced in 1942, was feared for its thick armor and powerful 88mm gun. While relatively slow and mechanically complex, it had a profound impact on Allied tank tactics and prompted the development of heavier Allied tanks in response.

6. Leopard 2: The German Leopard 2 main battle tank, introduced in the 1970s, is widely regarded as one of the finest tanks in the world. With its advanced armor protection, firepower, and mobility, it has been exported to numerous countries and remains in service today.

7. Challenger 2: The British Challenger 2 main battle tank, introduced in the late 1990s, is known for its exceptional armor protection and firepower. It has seen combat in Iraq and continues to serve as the backbone of the British Army's armored forces.

8. M1 Abrams: The American M1 Abrams main battle tank, introduced in the 1980s, is considered one of the most advanced and heavily armored tanks in the world. Its gas turbine engine, advanced fire control system, and composite armor make it a formidable opponent on the battlefield.

9. Panther: The German Panther medium tank, introduced in 1943, was designed to counter the Soviet T-34 and serve as a more mobile and versatile alternative to the Tiger I. Despite initial teething problems, it became one of the most iconic German tanks of World War II.

10. Type 99: The Japanese Type 99 main battle tank, introduced in the late 20th century, represents Japan's most modern tank design. With its advanced technology and firepower, it reflects Japan's efforts to maintain a capable armored force in the post-war era.

11. Cromwell: The British Cromwell cruiser tank, introduced during World War II, combined speed, firepower, and reliability in a highly mobile package. It played a significant role in the Allied push through Northwest Europe and subsequent campaigns against Nazi Germany.

12. AMX-30: The French AMX-30 main battle tank, introduced in the 1960s, represented a departure from traditional French tank design philosophy with its emphasis on speed and mobility. It saw service in conflicts such as the Gulf War and remained in French service until the 2010s.

13. T-72: The Soviet T-72 main battle tank, introduced in the 1970s, became one of the most widely produced tanks in the

world. With its relatively low cost, simplicity, and export success, it has seen extensive service in conflicts around the globe.

14. Type 59: The Chinese Type 59 main battle tank, introduced in the late 1950s, was based on the Soviet T-54A design and became the backbone of the People's Liberation Army's armored forces. It has been exported to numerous countries and remains in service today.

15. Sherman Firefly: The British Sherman Firefly variant, equipped with a powerful 17-pounder gun, served as a key Allied tank destroyer during World War II. Its ability to penetrate the armor of German heavy tanks made it a valuable asset in the fight against the Wehrmacht.

16. T-80: The Soviet T-80 main battle tank, introduced in the 1970s, was one of the first tanks to feature a gas turbine engine for propulsion. Despite its technological advancements, it faced challenges in terms of reliability and maintenance.

17. Churchill: The British Churchill infantry tank, introduced during World War II, was known for its heavy armor and ability to traverse difficult terrain. It played a crucial role in Allied operations in North Africa, Italy, and Northwest Europe.

18. Merkava: The Israeli Merkava main battle tank, introduced in the 1970s, was designed with a focus on crew survivability and

protection. Its unique rear-engine layout and emphasis on troop transport capabilities reflect Israel's strategic requirements and operational doctrine.

19. Matilda II: The British Matilda II infantry tank, introduced in the late 1930s, was heavily armored for its time and earned the nickname "Queen of the Desert" for its performance in North Africa. It proved to be a tough opponent for Axis forces during the early years of World War II.

20. Type 10: The Japanese Type 10 main battle tank, introduced in the 21st century, represents Japan's most advanced tank design to date. With its lightweight composite armor, advanced fire control system, and modular design, it reflects Japan's commitment to modernizing its armored forces.

3

ARMORED FEATS AND RECORD-BREAKING ADVANCES

1. The Battle of Kursk: The Battle of Kursk, fought in 1943 on the Eastern Front of World War II, saw the largest tank engagement in history. Hundreds of tanks clashed in a massive armored confrontation that ultimately resulted in a strategic victory for the Soviet Union.

2. The Crossing of the Rhine: During World War II, Allied forces executed Operation Plunder in March 1945, crossing the Rhine River into Germany. Armored divisions played a crucial role in the successful amphibious assault, overcoming formidable obstacles and securing vital bridgeheads.

3. The First Armored Divisions: The concept of the armored division, combining tanks, infantry, and artillery into a highly mobile and versatile force, emerged during World War II. The first armored divisions, such as the British 1st Armoured Division and the German 1st Panzer Division, pioneered armored warfare tactics and strategies.

4. The Desert Rats: The British 7th Armoured Division, known as the "Desert Rats," achieved fame and distinction for its actions in North Africa during World War II. Equipped with tanks such as the Crusader, Grant, and Sherman, the Desert Rats played a pivotal role in the campaigns against Axis forces in the desert.

5. The Blitzkrieg Doctrine: The German Blitzkrieg, or "lightning war," employed during World War II revolutionized armored warfare with its emphasis on speed, surprise, and combined arms tactics. Panzer divisions spearheaded offensives, swiftly bypassing enemy defenses and encircling opposing forces.

6. The Battle of Prokhorovka: Fought during the Battle of Kursk in 1943, the Battle of Prokhorovka witnessed one of the largest tank battles in history between German and Soviet armored forces. Despite fierce resistance, the Soviet Red Army successfully repelled German advances, inflicting heavy losses on enemy tanks.

7. The Ardennes Counteroffensive: During the Battle of the Bulge in December 1944, German forces launched a massive armored counteroffensive through the Ardennes forest. Despite initial successes, Allied resistance, including that of American armored units, halted the German advance and turned the tide of the battle.

8. The Gulf War Tank Battles: The Gulf War of 1990-1991 saw some of the largest tank battles since World War II, as Iraqi and Coalition armored forces clashed in the deserts of Kuwait and Iraq. American M1 Abrams tanks, British Challenger 1 tanks, and other modern armored vehicles played decisive roles in the conflict.

9. The Battle of Cambrai: Fought during World War I in November 1917, the Battle of Cambrai saw the first large-scale use of tanks in warfare. British Mark I tanks, supported by infantry and artillery, broke through German lines and achieved significant tactical gains before logistical issues halted their advance.

10. The Battle of El Alamein: The Battle of El Alamein in 1942 marked a turning point in the North African campaign of World War II. British and Commonwealth forces, including the 8th Armoured Brigade, defeated Axis forces and secured a decisive victory, paving the way for the Allied invasion of North Africa.

11. The Eastern Front Offensives: Soviet armored forces played a critical role in the massive offensives launched by the Red Army on the Eastern Front during World War II. Tanks such as the T-34 and KV-series played pivotal roles in breaking through German defenses and advancing deep into enemy territory.

12. The Battle of Arracourt: Fought in September 1944 during the Allied advance through France, the Battle of Arracourt saw

American armored units, including the 4th Armored Division, engage German panzer divisions in a series of intense tank battles. Despite being outnumbered, American tanks achieved a significant victory and halted German counterattacks.

13. The Warsaw Pact Armor: During the Cold War, the Warsaw Pact countries, led by the Soviet Union, maintained large armored forces equipped with tanks such as the T-72, T-64, and T-80. These tanks formed the backbone of Soviet and allied armies and were designed to counter NATO armored formations in a potential conflict.

14. The Battle of Gazala: Fought in May 1942 during the North African campaign of World War II, the Battle of Gazala saw German and Italian armored forces, led by Field Marshal Erwin Rommel, outmaneuver and encircle British and Commonwealth troops. Rommel's bold tactics and aggressive use of tanks contributed to Axis victory in the desert.

15. The Six-Day War Tank Battles: The Six-Day War of 1967 saw intense tank battles between Israeli and Arab forces in the Sinai Peninsula, West Bank, and Golan Heights. Israeli armored units, including the 7th Armored Brigade, achieved swift and decisive victories, capturing large swathes of territory and defeating enemy tanks in combat.

16. The Battle of Stalingrad: The Battle of Stalingrad, fought in 1942-1943, witnessed brutal urban combat and intense fighting between German and Soviet forces. Tanks, including the Soviet T-34 and German Panzer IV, played crucial roles in street fighting and close-quarters combat within the devastated city.

17. The Battle of Villers-Bocage: Fought in June 1944 during the Normandy campaign of World War II, the Battle of Villers-Bocage saw German Tiger tanks, commanded by SS-Obersturmführer Michael Wittmann, ambush and destroy a British armored column. Wittmann's tactical brilliance and aggressive actions became legendary in armored warfare history.

18. The Battle of 73 Easting: Fought during the Gulf War in 1991, the Battle of 73 Easting saw American armored forces, including the 2nd Armored Cavalry Regiment, decisively defeat Iraqi Republican Guard units in a swift and lopsided engagement. American M1 Abrams tanks demonstrated their superiority over Iraqi T-72s and other Soviet-era tanks.

19. The Battle of Brody: Fought in June 1941 during Operation Barbarossa, the German invasion of the Soviet Union, the Battle of Brody witnessed massive tank battles between German panzer divisions and Soviet mechanized corps. Despite initial Soviet successes, German armor eventually broke through Soviet lines, leading to the encirclement and destruction of large Soviet formations.

20. The Battle of Kasserine Pass: Fought in February 1943 during the North African campaign of World War II, the Battle of Kasserine Pass saw German and Italian forces inflict heavy losses on inexperienced American troops. The battle highlighted the importance of combined arms tactics and armored warfare training for Allied forces in the theater.

4

TANK TECHNOLOGY THROUGH THE AGES

1. The Invention of the Tank: The concept of the tank originated during World War I, with the British development of the Mark I tank in response to the challenges of trench warfare. Designed to cross enemy trenches and provide mobile firepower, early tanks revolutionized ground warfare.

2. Armor Innovations: Tank technology has continuously evolved to incorporate stronger and more effective armor materials. From the riveted steel armor of early tanks to the composite and reactive armor used in modern main battle tanks, advancements in armor technology have greatly enhanced crew protection on the battlefield.

3. Gun Evolution: Tank armaments have undergone significant evolution over the years. Early tanks were equipped with small-caliber guns or machine guns for infantry support, while modern main battle tanks boast powerful cannons capable of engaging enemy armor at long ranges with high accuracy.

4. Engine Development: Tanks have transitioned from early gasoline and diesel engines to more advanced powerplants, such as gas turbines and diesel-electric hybrids. These engines provide increased power output, improved fuel efficiency, and enhanced mobility on diverse terrain.

5. Suspension Systems: Suspension technology has played a crucial role in improving tank mobility and maneuverability. Early tanks utilized rudimentary suspension systems, while modern tanks feature sophisticated hydropneumatic or torsion bar suspensions, allowing for smoother rides over rough terrain.

6. Fire Control Systems: Advancements in fire control systems have enhanced the accuracy and lethality of tank armaments. Modern tanks are equipped with sophisticated targeting computers, thermal imaging sensors, and stabilized gun platforms, enabling accurate firing on the move and in adverse conditions.

7. Communication Systems: Effective communication is vital for coordinating tank movements and engaging enemy forces. Tank communication systems have evolved from basic radio sets to integrated networks that enable real-time data sharing and battlefield situational awareness among armored units.

8. NBC Protection: Nuclear, Biological, and Chemical (NBC) protection has become increasingly important in modern tank

design. Tanks are equipped with sealed crew compartments, filtration systems, and protective suits to shield crews from the hazards of NBC warfare.

9. Stealth Technology: Stealth technology has been incorporated into tank design to reduce their radar and infrared signatures, making them harder to detect and target on the battlefield. Features such as low-profile hulls, radar-absorbent materials, and heat-dissipating coatings help improve tank survivability in modern conflicts.

10. Autonomous Systems: The integration of autonomous systems, such as unmanned ground vehicles (UGVs) and drones, is a growing trend in tank technology. These systems can perform reconnaissance, target acquisition, and other tasks, reducing the workload on tank crews and enhancing overall combat effectiveness.

11. Hybrid Powertrains: Some modern tanks utilize hybrid powertrains combining traditional internal combustion engines with electric propulsion systems. These hybrid tanks offer improved fuel efficiency, reduced emissions, and enhanced stealth capabilities, making them well-suited for a variety of operational environments.

12. Modular Design: Modular tank designs allow for easy customization and upgrades to meet evolving battlefield

requirements. Tanks can be equipped with different weapon systems, armor packages, and mission-specific equipment, maximizing their versatility and adaptability in combat situations.

13. Active Protection Systems (APS): Active Protection Systems are designed to detect and intercept incoming threats, such as anti-tank missiles and rockets, before they reach the tank. APS employ countermeasures such as soft and hard kill systems to neutralize threats and protect tank crews from harm.

14. Urban Warfare Adaptations: Tanks have been adapted for urban warfare, with features such as urban camouflage, reinforced armor, and close-quarters combat capabilities. Urban warfare kits include additional protection for vulnerable areas, such as the sides and rear of the tank, to mitigate the risks of ambushes and improvised explosive devices (IEDs).

15. Electric Drive Systems: Electric drive systems offer several advantages over traditional mechanical transmissions, including improved reliability, reduced maintenance requirements, and enhanced power delivery to the tracks. Electric drive tanks are quieter and more efficient, making them well-suited for reconnaissance and stealth operations.

16. Crew Ergonomics: Modern tanks prioritize crew comfort and ergonomics to improve operational effectiveness and reduce

crew fatigue. Tanks feature adjustable seats, climate control systems, and ergonomic controls to enhance crew comfort during long missions.

17. Adaptive Camouflage: Adaptive camouflage systems use sensors and displays to mimic the surrounding environment, making tanks harder to detect visually and thermally. These systems can change the tank's appearance in real-time, blending seamlessly into different terrain types and environmental conditions.

18. Remote Weapon Stations (RWS): Remote Weapon Stations enable tanks to engage targets with machine guns and other weapons without exposing the crew to enemy fire. RWS are operated from within the tank's armored hull, providing enhanced protection for the crew while maintaining firepower and situational awareness.

19. Hydrogen Fuel Cells: Hydrogen fuel cell technology offers a clean and efficient alternative to traditional fossil fuel-powered tanks. Hydrogen tanks can be used to generate electricity, powering electric motors for propulsion and onboard systems, with water vapor as the only emission.

20. Directed Energy Weapons: Directed Energy Weapons, such as high-energy lasers and electromagnetic railguns, represent the future of tank armament. These weapons offer precision

targeting, unlimited ammunition, and rapid engagement capabilities, potentially revolutionizing armored warfare in the 21st century.

5

FAMOUS TANK COMMANDERS IN HISTORY

1. General Heinz Guderian: Known as the "Father of the Panzer Corps," Guderian played a pivotal role in developing and implementing Blitzkrieg tactics during World War II. His innovative approach to armored warfare emphasized speed, surprise, and decisive action, leading to numerous German victories in the early stages of the war.

2. General George S. Patton: Patton was one of the most prominent Allied tank commanders of World War II. His aggressive leadership style and strategic brilliance earned him the nickname "Old Blood and Guts." Patton commanded the U.S. Third Army during the Allied advance across Europe, leading successful armored offensives in key battles such as the Battle of the Bulge and the breakout from Normandy.

3. Field Marshal Erwin Rommel: Known as the "Desert Fox," Rommel gained fame for his command of the Afrika Korps during the North African campaign of World War II. A master of mobile warfare, Rommel orchestrated daring armored

maneuvers and surprise attacks against British and Commonwealth forces, earning the respect of both allies and adversaries.

4. Marshal Georgy Zhukov: Zhukov was a leading Soviet military commander during World War II, renowned for his strategic genius and tactical skill. As commander of the Red Army's Western Front, Zhukov played a key role in the defense of Moscow and the successful counteroffensive at Stalingrad, as well as the decisive victories at Kursk and Berlin.

5. General Philippe Leclerc: Leclerc was a French armored division commander who distinguished himself during World War II, particularly in the liberation of France. Leading the Free French 2nd Armored Division, Leclerc played a crucial role in the Battle of Normandy and the liberation of Paris, earning him widespread acclaim as a national hero.

6. Major-General Michael Wittmann: Wittmann was a highly decorated German tank commander known for his exceptional skill and bravery in combat. Commanding Tiger tanks, Wittmann achieved legendary status for his actions during the Battle of Villers-Bocage in Normandy, where he single-handedly destroyed numerous Allied vehicles and disrupted their advance.

7. Lieutenant-General Otto Carius: Carius was a German tank ace and recipient of the Knight's Cross of the Iron Cross with Oak

Leaves. Serving on the Eastern Front during World War II, Carius achieved over 150 confirmed tank kills, making him one of the most successful tank commanders in history.

8. Major-General Israel Tal: Tal was an Israeli armored warfare expert and commander who played a key role in the development of the Israeli Armored Corps. Known as the "father of the Merkava tank," Tal oversaw the design and production of Israel's indigenous main battle tank, which has since become a symbol of Israeli military prowess.

9. Lieutenant-Colonel Creighton Abrams: Abrams was an influential American tank commander who later served as Chief of Staff of the United States Army and Commander of U.S. Forces in Vietnam. During World War II, Abrams commanded the 37th Tank Battalion and played a significant role in the Allied liberation of Europe, earning the Distinguished Service Cross for his actions.

10. Colonel David R. Eshel: Eshel was an Israeli tank commander and military strategist who played a crucial role in the development of armored tactics and doctrine for the Israel Defense Forces (IDF). As commander of the 7th Armored Brigade during the Yom Kippur War, Eshel led successful counterattacks against Syrian forces, demonstrating the effectiveness of Israeli armored units in modern warfare.

11. General William Slim: Slim was a British military commander who led the British Fourteenth Army in the Burma Campaign during World War II. Known for his tactical brilliance and leadership under difficult conditions, Slim orchestrated the successful defense of India and subsequent Allied offensives against Japanese forces in Southeast Asia.

12. Lieutenant-General Vyacheslav Tsvetayev: Tsvetayev was a Soviet tank commander who distinguished himself during World War II, particularly in the Battle of Kursk. Leading the 1st Guards Tank Army, Tsvetayev played a crucial role in repelling German attacks and securing a decisive victory for the Red Army.

13. Major-General Adelbert Waldron: Waldron was an American tank commander and recipient of the Medal of Honor for his actions during the Vietnam War. Leading a tank platoon, Waldron bravely defended his position against overwhelming enemy forces, inflicting heavy casualties and preventing the capture of his unit.

14. Lieutenant-General Sir Brian Horrocks: Horrocks was a British tank commander who played a key role in the Allied victory in North Africa and Europe during World War II. Commanding the British XIII Corps, Horrocks led successful armored offensives in battles such as Operation Goodwood and Operation Market Garden, contributing to the defeat of Nazi Germany.

15. Colonel Yuri P. Kovalenko: Kovalenko was a Soviet tank commander and Hero of the Soviet Union who distinguished himself in numerous battles on the Eastern Front during World War II. Leading tank brigades and divisions, Kovalenko played a crucial role in breaking through German defenses and advancing deep into enemy territory.

16. Lieutenant-General Brian Kimmins: Kimmins was a British tank commander who served during World War II, commanding armored units in North Africa and Italy. Known for his tactical acumen and courage under fire, Kimmins played a significant role in the Allied victory in the Mediterranean theater, earning him the respect of his peers and superiors.

17. Lieutenant-General Sir Miles Dempsey: Dempsey was a British military commander who led the British Second Army during World War II. Playing a key role in the Normandy campaign and subsequent Allied offensives in Western Europe, Dempsey demonstrated exceptional leadership and tactical skill in coordinating armored and infantry units to achieve victory.

18. Major-General Otto von Knobelsdorff: Knobelsdorff was a German tank commander and recipient of the Knight's Cross of the Iron Cross with Oak Leaves and Swords. Leading panzer divisions on the Eastern Front, Knobelsdorff displayed

exceptional leadership and combat prowess, earning him recognition as one of Germany's top tank commanders.

19. Lieutenant-General Sir Oliver Leese: Leese was a British tank commander who served during World War II, commanding armored formations in North Africa and Italy. Known for his aggressive leadership style and willingness to take calculated risks, Leese played a significant role in the Allied victory in the Mediterranean theater.

20. Lieutenant-General Sir John Crocker: Crocker was a British tank commander who distinguished himself during World War II, particularly in the North African and Italian campaigns. Leading armored formations with skill and determination, Crocker played a crucial role in the Allied advance against Axis forces, contributing to the eventual defeat of Nazi Germany.

6

REMARKABLE TANK BATTLES AND CAMPAIGNS

1. Battle of Cambrai (1917): The first large-scale use of tanks in warfare, where British forces deployed nearly 500 tanks, breaking through German defenses and showcasing the potential of armored vehicles.

2. Battle of Kursk (1943): Known as the largest tank battle in history, involving over 6,000 tanks, 2 million troops, and 4,000 aircraft. The Soviet victory marked a turning point on the Eastern Front.

3. Battle of El Alamein (1942): A decisive Allied victory in North Africa, where British forces, under General Montgomery, defeated Rommel's Afrika Korps, marking the beginning of the end for Axis presence in Africa.

4. Battle of the Bulge (1944-1945): Germany's last major offensive in World War II, where over 1,000 tanks were involved. Despite initial success, the Allies eventually prevailed, depleting German resources.

5. Siege of Tobruk (1941-1942): An extended siege in North Africa where Australian forces defended the port of Tobruk against German and Italian forces, using tanks effectively in the defense.

6. Operation Goodwood (1944): A British offensive in Normandy involving 1,200 tanks aiming to break out from the Caen area. Despite heavy losses, it helped draw German forces away from the American sector.

7. Battle of Prokhorovka (1943): A significant clash within the Battle of Kursk, involving hundreds of Soviet and German tanks in close-quarters combat, resulting in heavy casualties on both sides.

8. Battle of Arracourt (1944): An engagement in France where American forces, despite being outnumbered, used superior tactics and coordination to defeat German tank units.

9. First Battle of Grozny (1994-1995): During the First Chechen War, Russian tanks faced intense urban combat, suffering heavy losses in the city's streets, highlighting the challenges of tanks in urban warfare.

10. Battle of 73 Easting (1991): A major tank battle during the Gulf War where American M1 Abrams tanks decimated Iraqi armored forces with superior technology and tactics.

11. Battle of Villers-Bocage (1944): Notable for German tank ace Michael Wittmann's ambush on British tanks, which temporarily halted the British advance in Normandy.

12. Battle of Hannut (1940): The first large-scale tank battle of World War II, fought between German and French armored units in Belgium. It demonstrated the importance of air support and coordination in armored warfare.

13. Battle of Sidi Bou Zid (1943): A clash in Tunisia where German forces, using superior tactics, inflicted a severe defeat on inexperienced American armored units.

14. Yom Kippur War (1973): Involving significant tank battles in the Sinai and Golan Heights, where Israeli tanks, despite initial setbacks, ultimately repelled Egyptian and Syrian forces.

15. Battle of Khafji (1991): The first major ground engagement of the Gulf War, where coalition forces, including tanks, repelled an Iraqi incursion into the Saudi Arabian town of Khafji.

16. Operation Market Garden (1944): An ambitious Allied operation in the Netherlands aiming to capture key bridges. Despite initial successes, the operation ultimately failed due to strong German resistance and logistical issues.

17. Battle of Chawinda (1965): Fought between India and Pakistan, it is one of the largest tank battles in the history of the subcontinent, with both sides deploying significant armored forces.

18. Battle of Basantar (1971): Another major tank battle between India and Pakistan during the Indo-Pakistani War of 1971, where Indian forces successfully crossed the Basantar River and repelled Pakistani counterattacks.

19. Battle of Berlin (1945): The final major offensive of World War II in Europe, where Soviet tanks played a crucial role in the capture of the German capital, leading to the end of the war in Europe.

20. Six-Day War (1967): Featured significant tank battles in the Sinai Desert and the Golan Heights, where Israeli armored units achieved rapid and decisive victories against Arab forces, changing the strategic landscape of the Middle East.

7

ACTS OF INNOVATION AND HEROISM IN ARMORED WARFARE

1. The Birth of the Tank: In 1916, during World War I, the British unveiled the first armored vehicle, the Mark I tank, revolutionizing warfare by introducing a new form of mobile, protected firepower on the battlefield.

2. The Strategic Brilliance of Blitzkrieg: Developed by General Heinz Guderian, Blitzkrieg tactics emphasized the coordinated use of tanks, infantry, and air support to achieve rapid and decisive victories, as demonstrated during the early stages of World War II.

3. The Battle of Cambrai: In 1917, British forces launched the first large-scale tank offensive in history at the Battle of Cambrai, showcasing the potential of armored vehicles to break through entrenched enemy lines and achieve strategic objectives.

4. Operation Desert Storm: During the Gulf War in 1991, coalition forces employed cutting-edge technology and innovative tactics, including precision-guided munitions and coordinated

air-ground operations, to achieve swift and decisive victories against Iraqi forces.

5. The Siege of Bastogne: In 1944, during the Battle of the Bulge, American forces defended the town of Bastogne against a massive German offensive, showcasing the resilience and determination of Allied troops in the face of overwhelming odds.

6. The Battle of Prokhorovka: Fought during the Battle of Kursk in 1943, the Battle of Prokhorovka saw Soviet and German tanks engage in one of the largest armored clashes in history, highlighting the ferocity and intensity of armored warfare on the Eastern Front.

7. The Development of Tank Doctrine: Throughout history, military leaders and theorists have continually refined tank doctrine, adapting tactics and strategies to maximize the effectiveness of armored units on the battlefield.

8. The Evolution of Tank Design: From the early, cumbersome tanks of World War I to the sophisticated main battle tanks of today, the evolution of tank design has been driven by advances in technology, armor protection, and firepower.

9. The Heroism of Tank Crews: Tank crews have consistently demonstrated courage, resilience, and camaraderie in the face of

adversity, often risking their lives to accomplish their missions and protect their fellow soldiers.

10. The Battle of Kursk: As the largest tank battle in history, the Battle of Kursk showcased the scale and ferocity of armored warfare on the Eastern Front, with hundreds of tanks engaging in intense combat over the course of several days.

11. The Doolittle Raid: In 1942, during World War II, American B-25 bombers launched a daring raid on Tokyo, demonstrating the potential of strategic bombing and boosting Allied morale in the wake of the Pearl Harbor attack.

12. The Battle of Midway: Fought in 1942, the Battle of Midway was a turning point in the Pacific Theater of World War II, with American carrier-based aircraft inflicting a decisive defeat on the Japanese navy and halting their advance in the Pacific.

13. The Desert Fox: Field Marshal Erwin Rommel, known as the "Desert Fox," was a master of armored warfare who achieved remarkable success in North Africa during World War II, demonstrating the importance of skillful leadership and tactical innovation on the battlefield.

14. The Battle of Stalingrad: As one of the largest and bloodiest battles in history, the Battle of Stalingrad highlighted the brutal

nature of urban warfare and the determination of Soviet forces to defend their city at all costs.

15. The Siege of Leningrad: Lasting for over 800 days during World War II, the Siege of Leningrad showcased the resilience and endurance of the Soviet people in the face of starvation, bombardment, and harsh winter conditions.

16. The Warsaw Uprising: In 1944, Polish resistance fighters launched the Warsaw Uprising against German occupation forces, demonstrating the courage and determination of the Polish people to fight for their freedom and independence.

17. The Battle of Guadalcanal: Fought in the Pacific Theater during World War II, the Battle of Guadalcanal was a grueling campaign marked by intense jungle fighting and amphibious assaults, showcasing the challenges of warfare in the Pacific islands.

18. The Battle of Okinawa: As one of the last major battles of World War II, the Battle of Okinawa was a brutal and protracted campaign that resulted in heavy casualties on both sides, foreshadowing the challenges of the impending invasion of Japan.

19. The Manhattan Project: The Manhattan Project was a top-secret research and development program during World War

II that resulted in the creation of the atomic bomb, showcasing the power of scientific innovation and technological advancement in warfare.

20. The Normandy Invasion: On June 6, 1944, Allied forces launched the largest amphibious invasion in history, landing on the beaches of Normandy to liberate Western Europe from Nazi occupation. The success of the Normandy Invasion marked a turning point in World War II and paved the way for the eventual defeat of Nazi Germany.

8

TANK TERMINOLOGY & JARGON

1. APFSDS (Armor-Piercing Fin-Stabilized Discarding Sabot): A type of kinetic energy penetrator ammunition designed to defeat modern armored vehicles, using a dart-like projectile that sheds its outer casing upon firing.

2. ERA (Explosive Reactive Armor): A type of armor that reacts explosively to the impact of an incoming projectile, neutralizing its penetration capabilities and enhancing the tank's survivability.

3. Glacis Plate: The sloped front armor plate of a tank, designed to deflect incoming rounds and increase the effective thickness of the armor.

4. Hatch: An entry or exit point on a tank, typically located on the turret or hull, allowing crew members to enter and exit the vehicle.

5. Hull: The main body of a tank, housing the engine, transmission, fuel, and crew compartments, providing the structural foundation for the vehicle.

6. Idler Wheel: A wheel at the front or rear of a tank's track system that maintains tension on the track and guides it around the running gear.

7. MBT (Main Battle Tank): A class of modern armored fighting vehicles characterized by heavy armor, powerful main guns, and versatile battlefield roles, such as the M1 Abrams or Leopard 2.

8. Reactive Armor: An advanced type of tank armor that detonates upon impact, mitigating the effects of enemy projectiles and enhancing the tank's protection.

9. Sabot: A device used to encase a smaller-diameter projectile, allowing it to be fired from a larger gun barrel and then discarding the casing upon leaving the barrel.

10. Sponson: The projecting side structure of a tank, often housing equipment, ammunition, or additional armor.

11. Track: The continuous band of treads that enables a tank to move across various terrains, distributing its weight and providing traction.

12. Turret: The rotating part of a tank that houses the main gun and sometimes secondary armaments, allowing for 360-degree targeting and engagement.

13. Cupola: A small, domed hatch on top of a tank turret, providing visibility and access for the tank commander or gunner.

14. Gun Mantlet: The armored shield that protects the base of a tank's main gun, allowing it to elevate and traverse while offering protection against incoming fire.

15. Commander's Override: A control system that allows the tank commander to take control of the turret and gun, overriding the gunner's controls in critical situations.

16. Rangefinder: A device used to determine the distance to a target, enabling accurate targeting and engagement by the tank's main gun.

17. HEAT (High-Explosive Anti-Tank): A type of ammunition designed to penetrate armor using a shaped charge explosive, effective against both armored vehicles and fortified positions.

18. Smoke Dischargers: Devices mounted on tanks that launch smoke grenades, creating a smoke screen to obscure the vehicle from enemy observation and targeting.

19. Tread: The individual segments of a tank's track, providing traction and distributing the vehicle's weight across a larger surface area.

20. Gun Depression/Elevation: The ability of a tank's main gun to angle downward (depression) or upward (elevation), allowing it to engage targets at various elevations relative to the tank's position.

9

EVOLUTION OF TANK DESIGN AND ARMOR

1. Mark I Tank (1916): The first-ever tank used in combat, developed by the British during World War I. It featured rhomboid tracks to cross trenches and barbed wire.

2. Christie Suspension (1928): An innovative suspension system developed by J. Walter Christie that allowed tanks to move faster and traverse rough terrain more effectively.

3. T-34 (1940): The Soviet T-34 revolutionized tank design with its sloped armor, which increased effective thickness and deflected incoming rounds, making it one of the most effective tanks of World War II.

4. Sherman Tank (1942): The American M4 Sherman was known for its reliability and ease of production. Over 49,000 units were produced, making it a staple of Allied armored forces.

5. Panther Tank (1943): A German medium tank that combined firepower, mobility, and protection. Its sloped armor and powerful 75mm gun made it one of the best tanks of World War II.

6. Composite Armor (1950s): Developed during the Cold War, composite armor combines multiple layers of different materials, such as metals and ceramics, to provide superior protection against various types of projectiles.

7. Chobham Armor (1960s): A type of composite armor developed in the UK, known for its excellent protection against both kinetic energy penetrators and shaped charges. It is used on tanks like the M1 Abrams and Challenger 2.

8. Reactive Armor (1970s): Explosive Reactive Armor (ERA) was introduced to enhance protection by using explosive charges to disrupt incoming projectiles, significantly improving survivability.

9. Leopard 2 (1979): The German Leopard 2 introduced advanced composite armor and a powerful 120mm smoothbore gun, setting new standards for modern main battle tanks.

10. M1 Abrams (1980): The American M1 Abrams featured advanced composite armor, a 120mm smoothbore gun, and a gas turbine engine, offering superior mobility and protection.

11. Active Protection Systems (2000s): Modern tanks are equipped with active protection systems (APS) like the Israeli Trophy, which detect and intercept incoming projectiles before they can hit the tank.

12. Stealth Technology (2010s): Efforts to reduce the radar and thermal signature of tanks have led to developments in stealth technology, making tanks less detectable to enemy sensors.

13. Modular Armor (2000s): Tanks like the Leopard 2A5 and later models feature modular armor, allowing damaged sections to be replaced or upgraded easily in the field.

14. Autoloaders (1960s): Developed to increase the rate of fire and reduce crew size, autoloaders are now common in many modern tanks, including the Russian T-72 and French Leclerc.

15. Armata T-14 (2015): The Russian T-14 Armata introduced an unmanned turret and advanced armor systems, representing a significant leap in tank design.

16. K2 Black Panther (2014): The South Korean K2 Black Panther features advanced composite armor, a 120mm smoothbore gun, and an autoloader, making it one of the most advanced tanks in the world.

17. Adaptive Camouflage (2010s): Research into adaptive camouflage aims to allow tanks to blend into their surroundings dynamically, improving battlefield survivability.

18. Hybrid Powertrains (2020s): Efforts to improve fuel efficiency and reduce logistical burdens have led to the development of hybrid powertrains for future tanks, combining diesel engines with electric motors.

19. Unmanned Tanks (2020s): Advances in robotics and AI are paving the way for unmanned tanks, which can operate autonomously or be remotely controlled, reducing risks to human crews.

20. Next-Generation Armor Materials (2020s): Ongoing research into new materials, such as graphene and advanced ceramics, promises to further enhance the protective capabilities of future tank armor.

10

CUTTING-EDGE TECHNOLOGY IN MODERN TANKS

1. Active Protection Systems (APS): Modern tanks like the Israeli Merkava and Russian Armata T-14 use APS to detect and intercept incoming anti-tank missiles and rockets before they hit the tank.

2. Unmanned Turrets: The Russian T-14 Armata features an unmanned turret, allowing the crew to stay protected within the heavily armored hull.

3. Advanced Fire Control Systems: Modern tanks are equipped with computerized fire control systems that calculate firing solutions in real-time, increasing accuracy and lethality.

4. Thermal Imaging: Thermal imaging technology allows tank crews to see through smoke, fog, and darkness, giving them a significant advantage in low-visibility conditions.

5. Laser Rangefinders: These devices measure the distance to a target with precision, improving the accuracy of the tank's main gun.

6. Autoloaders: Tanks like the French Leclerc and Russian T-90 use autoloaders to automatically load the main gun, reducing crew size and increasing the rate of fire.

7. Composite Armor: Modern composite armor, such as Chobham, provides superior protection against both kinetic energy penetrators and shaped charge warheads.

8. Remote Weapon Stations: These allow crew members to operate secondary weapons like machine guns and grenade launchers from within the safety of the tank.

9. Digital Battle Management Systems: Tanks are now integrated into digital networks, allowing for real-time communication, coordination, and data sharing with other units and command centers.

10. Laser Warning Receivers: These systems alert the crew when the tank is being targeted by laser-guided weapons, allowing them to take evasive action or deploy countermeasures.

11. Adaptive Camouflage: Future tanks may use adaptive camouflage technology to change their appearance to match their surroundings, making them harder to detect.

12. Hybrid Powertrains: Some modern tanks are exploring the use of hybrid powertrains, combining traditional diesel engines with electric motors to improve fuel efficiency and reduce heat signatures.

13. Multi-spectral Smoke Grenades: These grenades create a smoke screen that blocks not just visible light but also infrared and laser targeting systems, providing enhanced concealment.

14. High-Pressure Guns: Advanced tanks like the German Leopard 2A7+ feature high-pressure smoothbore guns capable of firing a variety of advanced munitions.

15. Situational Awareness Systems: These systems provide 360-degree surveillance around the tank, alerting the crew to potential threats from all directions.

16. Drone Integration: Some modern tanks are equipped with drones that can be deployed to scout the battlefield, providing valuable reconnaissance information.

17. Artificial Intelligence: AI is being integrated into tank systems for improved targeting, navigation, and decision-making processes.

18. Explosive Reactive Armor (ERA): ERA consists of explosive tiles that detonate on impact, disrupting incoming projectiles before they can penetrate the main armor.

19. Modular Armor: Tanks like the Leopard 2 can be fitted with modular armor packages that can be upgraded or replaced as needed, enhancing flexibility and adaptability.

20. Next-Generation Sensor Systems: Cutting-edge sensors can detect a wide range of threats, from anti-tank guided missiles to improvised explosive devices, enhancing the tank's defensive capabilities.

11

TANK TACTICS AND STRATEGIC MANEUVERS

1. Blitzkrieg Tactics: Developed by the Germans during World War II, Blitzkrieg, or "lightning war," emphasized fast-moving, coordinated attacks using tanks and aircraft to quickly overwhelm enemy defenses.

2. Flanking Maneuver: This tactic involves tanks moving around the sides of an enemy force to attack from the rear or sides, where armor is typically weaker.

3. Hull-Down Position: Tanks use the hull-down position to minimize exposure by hiding their hulls behind terrain features while keeping the turret and gun ready to fire.

4. Bounding Overwatch: In this tactic, one group of tanks advances while another group covers them, providing suppressive fire and protection from enemy attacks.

5. Encirclement: Tanks can be used to encircle enemy forces, cutting off their supply lines and escape routes, and forcing a surrender or destruction.

6. Pincer Movement: This strategy involves two tank forces attacking the enemy from opposite sides simultaneously, effectively trapping them in a pincer grip.

7. Breakthrough: Tanks concentrate their attack on a narrow front to penetrate enemy lines and disrupt their rear areas, leading to disorganization and retreat.

8. Leapfrogging: Similar to bounding overwatch, leapfrogging involves tanks advancing in stages, with some units moving forward while others provide cover, ensuring continuous protection and momentum.

9. Overwatch Fire: Tanks provide overwatch fire by positioning themselves in elevated positions to cover advancing infantry or other tanks, detecting and engaging threats from a distance.

10. Counterattack: When an enemy force breaches a defensive line, tanks can be used to launch a swift counterattack, exploiting the enemy's vulnerabilities and restoring the defensive position.

11. Urban Combat Tactics: In urban environments, tanks coordinate with infantry to navigate tight spaces and clear buildings, using their firepower to support infantry movements.

12. Feint Attacks: Tanks can perform feint attacks to deceive the enemy into concentrating their forces in one area while the main attack occurs elsewhere.

13. Ambush Tactics: Tanks can lie in wait in concealed positions to surprise and destroy passing enemy forces, leveraging their firepower and armor advantage.

14. Reconnaissance in Force: Tanks conduct aggressive reconnaissance missions to probe enemy defenses, gather intelligence, and engage enemy forces if necessary.

15. Mobile Defense: Tanks in mobile defense use their speed and firepower to hit and run, delaying and disrupting advancing enemy forces while avoiding direct engagement.

16. Defensive Perimeter: Tanks form a defensive perimeter around key positions or assets, creating a formidable barrier against enemy attacks.

17. Armored Spearhead: An armored spearhead involves a concentrated tank assault to create a breach in enemy defenses, allowing infantry and support units to follow through.

18. Deception Tactics: Tanks use camouflage, smoke screens, and dummy tanks to mislead the enemy about their true positions and intentions.

19. Fire and Maneuver: Tanks alternate between firing at the enemy and moving to new positions, making it difficult for the enemy to target them accurately.

20. Combined Arms Operations: Tanks work in conjunction with infantry, artillery, and aircraft to create a synergistic effect, maximizing the effectiveness of the combined force against the enemy.

12

ARMORED OPERATIONS AND LOGISTICS

1. Tank Transporters: Heavy-duty vehicles like the M1070 HET are designed to transport tanks over long distances, preventing wear and tear on the tank's tracks and engines.

2. Field Repair Units: During combat operations, specialized field repair units provide on-the-spot maintenance and repairs to keep tanks operational.

3. Ammunition Resupply: Tanks rely on a constant supply of ammunition, often delivered by logistics vehicles under combat conditions to ensure they remain ready for action.

4. Fuel Logistics: Modern tanks consume large amounts of fuel; logistical support units must ensure a steady supply, often using fuel trucks and pipelines.

5. Bridge Layers: Tanks like the M60 AVLB are equipped with deployable bridges, allowing armored units to cross rivers and other obstacles quickly.

6. Recovery Vehicles: Armored recovery vehicles (ARVs) like the M88 Hercules are used to tow damaged or disabled tanks back to safety for repairs.

7. Night Operations: Tanks equipped with night vision and infrared technology can operate effectively in low-light conditions, maintaining operational tempo 24/7.

8. Combat Engineers: These units support tank operations by clearing obstacles, building fortifications, and preparing routes for armored advances.

9. Supply Chains: Effective tank operations depend on well-coordinated supply chains, ensuring timely delivery of parts, fuel, and ammunition to the front lines.

10. Armored Convoys: Tanks often travel in armored convoys for mutual protection against ambushes and to ensure the delivery of critical supplies.

11. Mobility Corridors: Identifying and maintaining mobility corridors—areas where tanks can move freely—is crucial for successful armored operations.

12. Prepositioned Stocks: Armies maintain prepositioned stocks of tanks and supplies in strategic locations to enable rapid deployment in times of crisis.

13. Maintenance Cycles: Tanks undergo regular maintenance cycles to ensure peak performance, involving both preventative and corrective maintenance routines.

14. Command and Control: Effective armored operations require robust command and control systems to coordinate movements, logistics, and combat actions.

15. Mine Clearing: Specialized vehicles and units are tasked with clearing mines and other explosive obstacles from tank routes, ensuring safe passage.

16. Air Mobility: Some tanks and armored vehicles can be airlifted by transport aircraft like the C-17 Globemaster III, allowing rapid deployment to distant theaters.

17. Tank Crews: A tank crew typically includes a commander, gunner, loader, and driver, each with specific roles to ensure the tank operates smoothly.

18. Armored Doctrine: Armies develop armored doctrines that outline the principles and strategies for using tanks effectively in various combat scenarios.

19. Cold Weather Operations: Tanks are modified for cold weather operations with features like engine heaters and special lubricants to function in extreme temperatures.

20. Integrated Logistics Support: This comprehensive approach ensures that all aspects of logistics, from spare parts to training and support equipment, are integrated into tank operations for maximum efficiency.

13

DYNAMIC DUELS IN TANK WARFARE HISTORY

1. The Battle of Kursk: The largest tank battle in history, fought in 1943 between Nazi Germany and the Soviet Union, saw over 6,000 tanks clash in a titanic struggle on the Eastern Front.

2. El Alamein: In 1942, British and German tank forces faced off in the North African desert. The decisive British victory marked a turning point in the Western Desert Campaign.

3. Battle of the Bulge: During this 1944 battle, the Allies and Germans engaged in fierce tank combat in the Ardennes. The American M4 Sherman proved crucial in repelling the German offensive.

4. Prokhorovka: A part of the Battle of Kursk, the engagement at Prokhorovka saw the Soviet T-34s clashing with the German Tigers and Panthers in close-quarters tank combat.

5. The Battle of Arracourt: In September 1944, American M4 Shermans successfully countered a German counteroffensive in France, demonstrating superior tactics and coordination.

6. Operation Goodwood: In July 1944, British and Canadian forces launched a massive armored attack near Caen, France, involving over 1,200 tanks against well-entrenched German defenses.

7. The Golan Heights: During the 1973 Yom Kippur War, Israeli and Syrian tanks engaged in brutal battles on the Golan Heights. Israeli Centurions and Pattons outmaneuvered and outgunned Syrian T-55s and T-62s.

8. The Battle of the Cherkassy Pocket: In early 1944, German and Soviet tanks fought in the encirclement and breakout battle, highlighting the tactical prowess and resilience of both sides' armored units.

9. T-34 vs. Tiger at Villers-Bocage: In 1944, German tank ace Michael Wittmann and his Tiger tank famously ambushed and destroyed a column of British tanks and vehicles, demonstrating the power of the Tiger.

10. The Battle of Gazala: In 1942, German Afrika Korps tanks under Rommel outflanked and defeated British forces in Libya, leading to the capture of Tobruk.

11. Lake Balaton Offensive: In 1945, one of the last major German offensives saw heavy tank battles between German and Soviet forces around Lake Balaton in Hungary.

12. Battle of Chawinda: During the 1965 Indo-Pakistani War, one of the largest tank battles since World War II took place, with Pakistani and Indian armor clashing near Chawinda in Punjab.

13. The Battle of Basra: In the 2003 Iraq War, British Challenger 2 tanks played a key role in capturing the city of Basra from Iraqi forces, demonstrating superior technology and training.

14. Operation Desert Storm: In 1991, American M1 Abrams tanks outperformed Iraqi T-72s in the Gulf War, showcasing the effectiveness of modern Western armor and combined arms tactics.

15. The Battle of Sidi Bou Zid: In 1943, American tanks faced off against the Afrika Korps in Tunisia. Despite initial setbacks, lessons learned here would improve Allied armored tactics.

16. Battle of Brody: In 1941, one of the largest tank battles of World War II occurred in Ukraine, where Soviet and German tanks fought a chaotic and brutal engagement.

17. Operation Bagration: In 1944, Soviet tanks spearheaded a massive offensive that decimated German Army Group Centre,

showcasing the Red Army's growing proficiency in armored warfare.

18. Battle of Debrecen: In 1944, German and Hungarian forces engaged Soviet tanks in a mobile battle in Hungary, with significant armored engagements and maneuvers.

19. The Battle of Ramadi: During the Iraq War, American tanks, including M1 Abrams, played a crucial role in urban combat operations to retake the city from insurgents.

20. Battle of 73 Easting: In 1991, during the Gulf War, the U.S. 2nd Armored Cavalry Regiment decisively defeated Iraqi armored forces in a textbook example of superior tactics, technology, and training.

14

HUMOROUS ANECDOTES & SUPERSTITIONS IN ARMORED UNITS

1. Lucky Tank Hats: Many tank crews believe in wearing "lucky" hats or helmets during combat missions, convinced that these items bring good fortune and protect them from harm.

2. The Chocolate Tank: During World War II, British engineers built a tank disguised as a giant chocolate bar for a military parade, providing a moment of levity amidst the seriousness of war.

3. Naming Rituals: It's a common tradition for tank crews to give their tanks names, often humorous or fearsome, to create a bond with their armored vehicles. Names like "Big Bertha" or "Rolling Thunder" are popular choices.

4. Tank Commander's Teddy Bear: Some commanders keep a small teddy bear or other stuffed animal in their tank for good luck, a practice that has been passed down through generations of tankers.

5. The Unstoppable Sherman: An American Sherman tank named "Cobra King" became famous for being the first to break through German lines during the Battle of the Bulge, and its crew credited the tank's success to a lucky charm.

6. Superstitious Maintenance: Some tank crews have specific rituals they follow when performing maintenance on their tanks, believing that deviating from these rituals will bring bad luck or mechanical failure.

7. The Ghost Tank of the Desert: Legend has it that a ghostly tank roams the deserts of North Africa, a remnant of the fierce battles fought there during World War II. Sightings of the "Ghost Tank" are said to bring good luck to those who spot it.

8. Shoe Tossing Tradition: Before deploying, some tank crews throw an old shoe over their tank for good luck, a tradition believed to ward off bad luck and ensure a safe return.

9. Tank Baptism: New tanks often undergo a "baptism" where they are doused with water or champagne. This ritual is thought to bring good luck and a long, successful service life.

10. The Lucky Toolbox: Some crews carry a special toolbox that is believed to have magical properties, ensuring that any repairs made with its tools will be successful and long-lasting.

11. Pennies in the Tracks: A common superstition involves placing pennies or other small coins in the tank's tracks for good luck, ensuring smooth operation and protection in battle.

12. The Ghostly Handprint: Many tankers claim to have seen mysterious handprints appear on their tanks after battle. These handprints are believed to be the spirits of fallen comrades offering their protection.

13. Mascot Animals: Some tank units adopt small animals as mascots, such as cats or dogs, believing that these creatures bring good luck and boost morale.

14. The Unbroken Watch: A tank commander's watch that survives multiple battles without breaking is considered a powerful good luck charm, symbolizing the tank's resilience.

15. Whistling for Luck: Before heading into battle, some tank crews whistle a particular tune, believing it will bring them good luck and help them return safely.

16. Tank Graveyard Ghosts: It's said that tank graveyards, where old tanks are stored or scrapped, are haunted by the spirits of the tanks themselves, which sometimes come to life and move on their own.

17. The Never-Washed Tank: Some crews believe that washing their tank will wash away its luck, so they avoid cleaning it, especially before important missions.

18. Combat Rations Ritual: A common superstition is that the last combat ration left in a tank is never eaten, as doing so would bring bad luck and ensure that the crew runs out of supplies.

19. Tank Whispers: Tankers often talk to their tanks, whispering encouragement and praise, believing that this fosters a better "relationship" with the vehicle and improves its performance.

20. The Phantom Crew Member: There are tales of an invisible crew member who appears in tanks during fierce battles, providing an extra pair of hands to help the crew and then disappearing without a trace.

15

TRIUMPHS AND CHALLENGES IN TANK DEVELOPMENT

1. The Birth of the Tank: The first tanks, such as the British Mark I, debuted in World War I, marking a revolutionary step in warfare by overcoming trench obstacles and providing mobile firepower.

2. Armor Evolution: Early tanks had thin armor, vulnerable to enemy fire. Over time, advancements in metallurgy led to thicker, more resilient armor capable of withstanding powerful anti-tank weapons.

3. The Christie Suspension: Invented by American engineer J. Walter Christie, this suspension system allowed tanks to move faster and more smoothly over rough terrain, significantly enhancing their mobility.

4. T-34 Triumph: The Soviet T-34 tank, with its sloped armor and powerful 76.2mm gun, was considered one of the most effective tanks of World War II, playing a crucial role in the defeat of Nazi Germany.

5. Tiger Tank Challenges: The German Tiger I tank was a formidable machine with heavy armor and a powerful gun. However, its complexity, high production cost, and mechanical reliability issues posed significant challenges.

6. Sherman Adaptability: The American M4 Sherman tank was not the most heavily armored or armed, but its mechanical reliability, ease of production, and adaptability made it a crucial asset in World War II.

7. Composite Armor Innovation: The development of composite armor, such as Chobham armor, provided modern tanks with enhanced protection against both kinetic and shaped charge attacks.

8. Leopard 2 Excellence: The German Leopard 2 tank, renowned for its accuracy, firepower, and advanced armor protection, set new standards in tank design and remains one of the best tanks in the world.

9. Reactive Armor Breakthrough: Reactive armor, which explodes outward when hit, significantly improved tank survivability against shaped charges and rocket-propelled grenades.

10. Abrams Agility: The American M1 Abrams tank, equipped with a powerful gas turbine engine, advanced armor, and

sophisticated fire control systems, demonstrated remarkable agility and firepower.

11. Amphibious Tanks: Some tanks, like the Soviet PT-76, were designed to operate in water, enabling amphibious assaults and adding a new dimension to armored warfare.

12. Night Vision Technology: The incorporation of night vision and thermal imaging technology allowed tanks to operate effectively in low visibility conditions, giving them a significant tactical advantage.

13. Drone Integration: Modern tanks are being equipped with drone systems for reconnaissance and targeting, extending their battlefield awareness and strike capabilities.

14. Light Tank Revival: The development of advanced materials and technology has led to a revival of light tanks, which offer speed and versatility for rapid deployment and reconnaissance missions.

15. Urban Warfare Adaptations: Tanks have been adapted for urban warfare with additional armor, remote weapon stations, and advanced sensors to navigate and fight effectively in built-up areas.

16. Tank Autonomy: Research and development are ongoing into autonomous tanks, which could operate without a crew, reducing human risk and potentially transforming future armored warfare.

17. Hybrid Power Systems: The exploration of hybrid-electric power systems for tanks aims to reduce fuel consumption, enhance stealth, and provide additional electrical power for advanced systems.

18. Tank Weight Challenges: As tanks became heavier due to increased armor and weaponry, challenges in transportation and deployment emerged, requiring innovative logistical solutions.

19. Modular Design Advantage: Modern tanks are often designed with modular components, allowing for easier upgrades and repairs, and enabling tanks to be quickly adapted for various missions.

20. Future Prospects: The ongoing development of next-generation tanks focuses on integrating artificial intelligence, advanced materials, and cutting-edge weaponry to maintain superiority on the battlefield.

16

CAMARADERIE AMONG TANK CREWS

1. Close-Knit Teams: Tank crews often form close bonds due to the intense and confined nature of their work, fostering a strong sense of camaraderie and trust.

2. Shared Responsibilities: Each crew member has specific roles, such as driver, gunner, loader, and commander, and they must work seamlessly together to ensure the tank operates effectively.

3. Communication Mastery: Effective communication is crucial in a tank, with crews developing their own shorthand and signals to convey critical information quickly.

4. Living Conditions: The cramped conditions inside a tank mean that crews often live and sleep in the vehicle for extended periods, reinforcing their reliance on one another.

5. Crew Training: Tank crews undergo rigorous training together, learning to operate the tank as a single unit and building strong interpersonal connections.

6. Unit Cohesion: Successful tank units often attribute their effectiveness to the strong cohesion and mutual respect among crew members, which enhances their performance in combat.

7. Trust Under Fire: In battle, crew members must trust each other implicitly, knowing that their lives depend on the skill and quick reactions of their teammates.

8. Shared Hardships: Enduring difficult conditions, such as extreme weather and long missions, strengthens the bond among crew members, creating a sense of brotherhood.

9. Rituals and Traditions: Tank crews often develop their own rituals and traditions, from naming their tanks to creating unit-specific insignias, which foster a sense of identity and pride.

10. Celebrating Successes: After successful missions, crews often celebrate together, reinforcing their bonds and boosting morale.

11. Handling Loss: When a crew member is lost, the impact is profound, but the shared grief often brings the remaining members even closer together.

12. Problem-Solving: Working in a tank requires constant problem-solving and innovation, and the ability to collaborate effectively is key to overcoming challenges.

13. Humor as a Coping Mechanism: Humor is often used by tank crews to cope with the stress and danger of their missions, helping to maintain morale.

14. Veteran Stories: Many veteran tank crews share stories of their experiences, highlighting the unique bond formed through their service.

15. Training Exercises: Joint training exercises with other tank crews can create friendly rivalries and foster a wider sense of camaraderie within the armored units.

16. Post-Service Connections: The bonds formed in tank crews often last beyond military service, with many former crew members staying in touch and supporting each other in civilian life.

17. Adaptation to Roles: Crews often rotate roles to ensure everyone is proficient in multiple tasks, which builds a deeper understanding and respect for each position.

18. Shared Risks: The inherent dangers of tank operations mean that crew members are acutely aware of the risks they share, which strengthens their unity.

19. Support Networks: The families of tank crew members often form their own support networks, adding another layer of community and camaraderie.

20. Legacy and Heritage: Tank units often celebrate their history and heritage, passing down stories and traditions that honor the contributions and sacrifices of past crews.

17

UNFORGETTABLE MOMENTS IN TANK WARFARE HISTORY

1. Battle of Cambrai (1917): The first large-scale use of tanks in history occurred during the Battle of Cambrai in World War I, where British forces employed over 400 tanks to achieve a significant breakthrough in German lines.

2. The Charge of the Light Brigade (1918): During World War I, the British Tank Corps conducted a daring attack known as the Charge of the Light Brigade, where they penetrated deep into enemy territory, showcasing the potential of armored warfare.

3. The Battle of Kursk (1943): The Battle of Kursk, the largest tank battle in history, saw German and Soviet forces clash in a massive armored engagement, with over 6,000 tanks involved on each side.

4. Operation Citadel: Operation Citadel, the German offensive at Kursk, marked the first time Tiger tanks were used in combat, showcasing their formidable firepower and armor.

5. D-Day Landings (1944): On D-Day, Allied forces deployed specialized amphibious tanks, such as the Sherman DD, to support the infantry landings and overcome coastal defenses.

6. The Battle of the Bulge (1944): During the Battle of the Bulge, German Tiger II tanks, nicknamed "King Tigers," engaged in fierce combat against Allied forces, demonstrating their fearsome reputation on the battlefield.

7. The Battle of Prokhorovka (1943): The Battle of Prokhorovka, a pivotal engagement during the Battle of Kursk, saw thousands of tanks clash in a brutal confrontation that decided the fate of the German offensive.

8. The Siege of Bastogne (1944): American Sherman tanks played a crucial role in defending the town of Bastogne during the Battle of the Bulge, withstanding relentless German assaults and helping to repel the enemy.

9. The Desert War (1940s): Tank battles in North Africa, such as the engagements at El Alamein, showcased the importance of mobility and logistics in desert warfare, with both Allied and Axis forces employing tanks in vast desert landscapes.

10. The Battle of Stalingrad (1942-1943): Tanks played a significant role in the Battle of Stalingrad, with Soviet T-34s

engaging in fierce urban combat against German forces, contributing to the eventual Soviet victory.

11. The Warsaw Pact Invasion of Czechoslovakia (1968): Soviet tanks, including the T-55 and T-72, were deployed during the Warsaw Pact invasion of Czechoslovakia, demonstrating the continued importance of armored forces in Cold War conflicts.

12. The Yom Kippur War (1973): The Yom Kippur War saw intense tank battles between Israeli and Arab forces, including the iconic engagements in the Sinai Desert and on the Golan Heights, highlighting the evolving tactics and technology of armored warfare.

13. The Gulf War (1991): The Gulf War witnessed the introduction of advanced tanks such as the American M1 Abrams and British Challenger 1, which dominated the battlefield with their superior firepower and armor protection.

14. The Battle of 73 Easting (1991): During the Gulf War, the Battle of 73 Easting showcased the overwhelming superiority of American armored forces, as they decisively defeated Iraqi tank units in a rapid and lopsided engagement.

15. Operation Iraqi Freedom (2003): The invasion of Iraq in 2003 saw the extensive use of tanks, including the Abrams, in urban

combat and maneuver warfare, demonstrating the continued relevance of armored forces in modern conflicts.

16. The Battle of Grozny (1994-1995): Russian tanks, including the T-72 and BMP infantry fighting vehicles, faced intense urban combat during the First Chechen War, highlighting the challenges of armored warfare in built-up areas.

17. The Battle of Khafji (1991): The Battle of Khafji during the Gulf War saw Saudi and coalition forces engage in fierce tank battles against Iraqi armored units, demonstrating the importance of combined arms tactics and air support.

18. The Battle of Cuito Cuanavale (1987-1988): The largest tank battle in Africa since World War II occurred during the Angolan Civil War, with Cuban and Angolan forces engaging South African armored units in a protracted and bloody conflict.

19. The Battle of Hampton Roads (1862): The clash between the ironclad warships USS Monitor and CSS Virginia during the American Civil War marked a turning point in naval warfare, inspiring the development of armored vehicles, including tanks, in future conflicts.

20. The Battle of Suomussalmi (1939-1940): During the Winter War between Finland and the Soviet Union, Finnish ski troops and anti-tank units inflicted heavy casualties on Soviet armored

forces, demonstrating the effectiveness of innovative tactics against superior numbers.

18

INNOVATIONS THAT REVOLUTIONIZED ARMORED WARFARE

1. Turret Design: The introduction of the rotating turret, pioneered by the British in World War I with the Mark I tank, allowed tanks to engage targets in all directions without repositioning the entire vehicle.

2. Radio Communications: The integration of radio communication systems in tanks allowed for real-time coordination between units, improving battlefield awareness and facilitating tactical maneuvers.

3. Sloped Armor: Sloped armor, first employed on tanks like the Soviet T-34, increased protection by deflecting incoming projectiles, enhancing survivability on the battlefield.

4. Main Battle Tanks: The concept of the main battle tank, exemplified by designs like the American M1 Abrams and the Soviet T-72, combined mobility, firepower, and armor protection into a single versatile platform, revolutionizing armored warfare.

5. Gasoline Engines: The adoption of gasoline engines in early tanks provided greater mobility compared to earlier steam-powered designs, enabling tanks to operate more effectively in combat.

6. Composite Armor: Composite armor, incorporating layers of different materials such as ceramics and metals, offers enhanced protection against a variety of threats, from kinetic penetrators to shaped charges.

7. Gyroscopic Stabilization: Gyroscopic stabilization systems, introduced in tanks like the British Centurion, reduced the effects of recoil during firing, improving accuracy and allowing for accurate shooting on the move.

8. Fire Control Systems: Advanced fire control systems, integrating rangefinders, ballistic computers, and stabilization systems, greatly increased the accuracy and lethality of tank weapons.

9. Reactive Armor: Reactive armor tiles, which detonate upon impact to disrupt incoming projectiles, provide additional protection against shaped charge warheads, improving tank survivability.

10. Gas Turbine Engines: Gas turbine engines, utilized in tanks like the M1 Abrams, offer high power-to-weight ratios and increased reliability, enhancing mobility and operational range.

11. Hydraulic Suspension: Hydraulic suspension systems, such as those found in the Leopard 2 tank, provide improved ride comfort and stability over rough terrain, enhancing crew effectiveness and reducing fatigue.

12. Thermal Imaging Systems: Thermal imaging systems, mounted on tanks like the Challenger 2, allow for enhanced visibility in low-light conditions, providing a significant tactical advantage on the battlefield.

13. Remote Weapon Stations: Remote weapon stations, equipped with sensors and cameras, enable tank crews to engage targets while remaining under armor protection, increasing crew survivability.

14. Active Protection Systems: Active protection systems, such as the Israeli Trophy system, detect and intercept incoming projectiles before they can strike the tank, offering additional protection against anti-tank threats.

15. Modular Armor: Modular armor systems, allowing for the rapid replacement or upgrade of armor modules, enable tanks to adapt to evolving threats and operational requirements.

16. Air Conditioning Systems: Air conditioning systems installed in modern tanks improve crew comfort and combat effectiveness in hot climates, reducing fatigue and heat stress during prolonged operations.

17. Integrated Networking: Integrated networking capabilities, connecting tanks to other vehicles and command centers, enhance situational awareness and facilitate coordinated operations on the battlefield.

18. Crew Ergonomics: Ergonomic design features, such as adjustable seats and control layouts, improve crew comfort and efficiency during long missions, reducing fatigue and improving overall performance.

19. Laser Warning Systems: Laser warning systems, detecting incoming laser-guided threats, provide crews with early warning of potential attacks, allowing for timely defensive measures.

20. Autoloader Mechanisms: Autoloader mechanisms, found in tanks like the Russian T-14 Armata, automate the loading of ammunition, reducing crew workload and increasing the rate of fire in combat situations.

19

ARTISTIC REPRESENTATIONS OF TANKS IN CULTURE

1. Film and Television: Tanks have been featured prominently in countless films and TV shows, from classic war movies like "Saving Private Ryan" to futuristic sci-fi epics like "Starship Troopers."

2. Literature: Tanks have inspired authors to explore themes of warfare, technology, and human resilience in novels such as "The Tank Lords" by David Drake and "Fury" by Jim Frederick.

3. Music: Tanks have been referenced in numerous songs across various genres, from heavy metal anthems like "Tank" by The Stranglers to hip-hop tracks like "Tank!" by Cowboy Bebop.

4. Artwork: Tanks have been depicted in paintings, drawings, and sculptures by artists seeking to capture their imposing presence and significance in modern warfare.

5. Comics and Graphic Novels: Tanks often make appearances in comic books and graphic novels, serving as formidable adversaries or powerful symbols of military might.

6. Video Games: Tanks feature prominently in video games, from realistic tank simulators like "War Thunder" to action-packed shooters like "Battlefield" and "Call of Duty."

7. Fashion: Tank motifs have found their way into fashion, with tank-themed clothing and accessories appealing to enthusiasts and military aficionados alike.

8. Street Art: Tanks have been depicted in murals and graffiti art, sometimes as symbols of resistance or protest against war and militarism.

9. Photography: Tanks have been captured in striking photographs, both on the battlefield and in more peaceful settings, showcasing their imposing presence and technological complexity.

10. Sculpture: Tank sculptures, often created from metal or other industrial materials, can be found in public spaces as monuments to military history or symbols of strength and resilience.

11. Poetry: Tanks have been the subject of poetry, with poets exploring themes of warfare, heroism, and the human cost of conflict through evocative verse.

12. Digital Art: Tanks have been reimagined in digital art, with artists using computer graphics and animation to create stunning and dynamic representations of armored vehicles.

13. Tattoos: Tank tattoos are popular among military personnel and enthusiasts, with designs ranging from realistic depictions of specific tank models to more stylized and symbolic interpretations.

14. Model Kits: Tank model kits are a favorite hobby for many enthusiasts, allowing them to recreate their favorite tanks in miniature form with meticulous attention to detail.

15. Literary Criticism: Tanks have been analyzed and interpreted in academic studies and literary criticism, examining their cultural significance and representation in various forms of media.

16. Documentaries: Tanks have been the subject of numerous documentaries, providing insight into their history, technology, and role in shaping military conflicts throughout the 20th and 21st centuries.

17. War Memorials: Tanks are often featured in war memorials and monuments dedicated to honoring the sacrifices of soldiers and commemorating significant battles and campaigns.

18. Children's Books: Tanks are sometimes featured in children's books and educational materials, introducing young readers to the history and mechanics of armored vehicles in an accessible and engaging way.

19. Performance Art: Tanks have been incorporated into performance art pieces, with artists using them as symbols of power, destruction, and the human condition in live performances and installations.

20. Fan Art: Tanks inspire fan artists to create original artworks, fan fiction, and other creative expressions of their love for these iconic war machines, shared and celebrated within online communities and fan conventions.

20

THE FUTURE OF TANKS - TRENDS AND INNOVATIONS

1. Autonomous Operation: The future of tanks may see increased autonomy, with advancements in artificial intelligence enabling tanks to operate with minimal human intervention, potentially revolutionizing tactics and strategy on the battlefield.

2. Electric Propulsion: Electric propulsion systems offer the potential for quieter, more fuel-efficient tanks with reduced heat signatures, enhancing stealth and operational effectiveness in modern warfare scenarios.

3. Directed Energy Weapons: The development of directed energy weapons, such as lasers and particle beams, could provide tanks with unparalleled firepower and precision, capable of engaging multiple targets simultaneously with minimal collateral damage.

4. Active Protection Systems: Future tanks may feature even more advanced active protection systems, incorporating multiple layers of defense to counter a wide range of threats, from incoming missiles to enemy drones.

5. Modular Design: Modular tank designs could allow for rapid reconfiguration and adaptation to different mission requirements, enabling tanks to fulfill a variety of roles on the battlefield with greater flexibility and efficiency.

6. Enhanced Survivability: Advances in armor materials and design techniques may result in tanks with unprecedented levels of protection, capable of withstanding increasingly sophisticated anti-tank threats while minimizing weight and size constraints.

7. Swarm Tactics: Future tanks may operate in coordinated swarms, leveraging networked communications and autonomous capabilities to overwhelm enemy defenses and achieve tactical superiority on the battlefield.

8. Biometric Integration: Biometric sensors and interfaces could enhance crew performance and situational awareness, monitoring vital signs and cognitive states to optimize decision-making and combat effectiveness in high-stress environments.

9. Stealth Technology: Stealth technologies, including radar-absorbing materials and shape optimization, may enable tanks to reduce their radar cross-section and infrared signature, enhancing survivability against detection and targeting systems.

10. Underwater Capabilities: Future tanks may incorporate amphibious and underwater capabilities, allowing them to operate in diverse environments and traverse natural obstacles such as rivers and marshes with ease.

11. Energy Efficiency: Advances in energy storage and management could lead to more energy-efficient tanks, extending operational range and reducing logistical burdens in extended military campaigns.

12. Adaptive Camouflage: Tanks equipped with adaptive camouflage systems could dynamically adjust their appearance to blend seamlessly into different terrain types and environmental conditions, enhancing concealment and survivability.

13. Electrothermal-Chemical Propulsion: Electrothermal-chemical propulsion systems offer the potential for increased muzzle velocity and range, providing tanks with greater firepower and lethality against armored targets.

14. Non-Lethal Weapons: Non-lethal weapons, such as directed energy devices and acoustic deterrents, could provide tanks with additional options for crowd control and non-combat operations in urban environments and peacekeeping missions.

15. Biomechanical Enhancements: Biomechanical enhancements, including exoskeletons and neural interfaces, could augment crew strength and cognitive abilities, enhancing overall performance and endurance during extended missions.

16. Environmental Adaptation: Future tanks may be designed to operate in extreme environments, from arctic tundra to desert dunes, utilizing advanced cooling and heating systems to maintain optimal performance and crew comfort.

17. Modular Weapon Systems: Modular weapon systems could enable tanks to rapidly switch between different types of armaments, from conventional cannons to missile launchers, depending on mission requirements and threat assessments.

18. Hypersonic Mobility: Hypersonic propulsion technologies could enable tanks to achieve unprecedented speeds and maneuverability, reducing response times and increasing battlefield agility in dynamic combat situations.

19. Nano-Scale Materials: Nano-scale materials, such as carbon nanotubes and graphene, could revolutionize armor design, offering unparalleled strength and durability while minimizing weight and thickness constraints.

20. Human-Machine Integration: Future tanks may feature enhanced human-machine integration, with crew members

seamlessly interfacing with onboard systems and sensors to process vast amounts of information and make split-second decisions in combat situations.

CONCLUSION

As we reach the end of our journey through the captivating world of tanks in "400+ Thrilling & Unbelievable Tank Facts for Military Enthusiasts," it's time to reflect on the incredible impact these armored vehicles have had on military history and the human experience of warfare. This book has been your companion, illuminating the triumphs, challenges, and unforgettable moments that have defined the evolution of tank warfare.

Throughout these chapters, we've explored the diverse facets of armored warfare, from the groundbreaking innovations that revolutionized the battlefield to the legendary commanders who left their mark on history. We've marveled at the iconic tank models and their variants, the remarkable feats of bravery and ingenuity, and the unbreakable bonds forged among tank crews in the face of adversity.

The 400+ facts, stories, and anecdotes woven into these pages serve as a testament to the enduring fascination tanks hold for military enthusiasts and history buffs alike. Through these tales of heroism, innovation, and camaraderie, we've gained a deeper appreciation for the crucial role tanks have played in shaping the course of conflicts and the lives of those who have operated them.

As you close this book, remember that the story of tanks is far from over. With new technological advancements and evolving battlefield dynamics, the future of armored warfare promises to be just as exciting and transformative as its past. The lessons learned from the triumphs and challenges of tank history will undoubtedly shape the designs, strategies, and tactics of tomorrow's armored forces.

To the military enthusiasts, history buffs, and curious readers who have journeyed through these pages: know that your interest and appreciation for these incredible machines contribute to keeping their legacy alive. By exploring the rich history and ongoing developments in the world of tanks, you play a part in honoring the sacrifices and achievements of the brave men and women who have served in armored units throughout the years.

So, as you reflect on the fascinating world of tanks, carry with you the knowledge, insights, and sense of wonder gained from "400+ Thrilling & Unbelievable Tank Facts for Military Enthusiasts." Embrace the lessons of the past, the marvels of the present, and the exciting possibilities that await in the future of armored warfare.

Thank you for joining us on this thrilling exploration of the world of tanks. May the facts, stories, and trivia from these pages stay with you, sparking further curiosity and a deeper appreciation for the incredible machines that have left an indelible mark on military history.

The world of tanks continues to evolve, and the adventures that lie ahead are sure to be filled with innovation, bravery, and the unbreakable spirit of those who dedicate their lives to serving in armored units. So, keep exploring, keep learning, and never lose your fascination for these awe-inspiring machines and the remarkable individuals who operate them.

Author Note

Writing "400+ Thrilling & Unbelievable Tank Facts for Military Enthusiasts" has been an exhilarating and enlightening journey. As a lifelong military history enthusiast, I've always been captivated by the incredible impact of armored vehicles on the battlefield, the bravery of the men and women who operate them, and the ongoing innovations that continue to shape the future of tank warfare. This book has allowed me to share my passion for these awe-inspiring machines with fellow enthusiasts and to showcase the many ways in which tanks have influenced the course of military history.

Throughout the process of researching and curating the facts, stories, and anecdotes that comprise this book, I found myself continually in awe of the ingenuity, courage, and dedication displayed by tank designers, commanders, and crews throughout the years. From the early pioneers who first introduced tanks to the battlefield to the modern-day innovators pushing the boundaries of armored technology, each development serves as a testament to human perseverance and our innate desire to overcome challenges and protect those who serve.

It is my sincere hope that "400+ Thrilling & Unbelievable Tank Facts for Military Enthusiasts" not only informs and entertains but also inspires a deeper appreciation for the crucial role tanks have played in shaping military history. May the stories of innovation, heroism, and camaraderie contained within these pages serve as a tribute to the brave individuals who have dedicated their lives to serving in armored units and a reminder of the ongoing importance of these incredible machines.

To the military enthusiasts, history buffs, and readers with a thirst for knowledge who have explored the pages of this book: thank you for your shared passion and curiosity. Your interest in the world of tanks helps keep the legacy of these remarkable vehicles and the people who operate them alive, ensuring that their stories and sacrifices are never forgotten.

And to the brave men and women who have served or currently serve in armored units around the world: your courage, dedication, and skill are an inspiration to us all. The advancements in tank technology and the evolution of armored warfare tactics are a testament to your unwavering commitment to protecting others and serving your nations with honor.

Thank you for allowing me to share my fascination for the world of tanks with you through the pages of this book. I hope that "400+ Thrilling & Unbelievable Tank Facts for Military Enthusiasts" serves as a source of knowledge, entertainment, and appreciation for these incredible machines and the remarkable individuals who have shaped their history.

Wishing you all the best in your ongoing exploration of the captivating world of tanks,

Ethan Blackwell